About the Author

Open minded Pharmacist (Class of '95, Kings College, London), human, and earth lover, who relishes the desire to bring people together from all over the world through her word art. Her wish is for the language of love to be translated into daily actions. Walk with her through reading her word art, discover your own words and share your love for humanity and mother earth. She is inspired by English, Asian Poets from Rumi to Rossetti, as well as poems pertaining to meditation. She aims to amplify and project emotions which make us strong and vulnerable in life.

Love Rhapsodies

Fareeda Steele

Love Rhapsodies

Olympia Publishers
London

www.olympiapublishers.com
OLYMPIA PAPERBACK EDITION

A CIP catalogue record for this title is
available from the British Library.

ISBN: 978-1-80439-401-4

First Published in 2023

Olympia Publishers
Tallis House
2 Tallis Street
London
EC4Y 0AB

Printed in Great Britain

Dedication

I dedicate this book to our mother earth and all living things: big and small, and my loving family, who supports and bends like bamboo for me. My son, Kareem and daughter, Anisah, who are like my sun and moon. I dedicate Love Rhapsodies to my extended family of friends, pharmacists, researchers, doctors, nurses, psychotherapists, caregivers and teachers who adapted during the pandemic. I dedicate my writing to all farmers and cultivators of the land, who work tirelessly to make our landscapes beautiful and grow food for our tables. I hope many of my children and yours embrace the walk through the mindful garden and unlock their true spiritual potential.

Acknowledgements

I acknowledge all teachers and professors who openly discuss literary works. This allows a space where emotions and opinions can be freed. I acknowledge my daughter, an avid writer she was an opinion editor at the age of sixteen, Anisah Steele at Marjory Stoneman Douglas High School, Parkland, Florida. The school publication, The Eagle Eye, helped her express feelings as she suffered through the trauma of the school shooting fourteenth February 2018. Thanks to Marco Nozicka, LCSW and Life Coach at LifeWorks Inc, a lover of humanity, who helped to nurture word art in my thoughts. Through his help, my creative energy has been allowed to truly flourish. Avid reader Xian-Ming Zeng, PhD, and appreciator of poems encouraged me to keep writing during the pandemic. Through Zeng's steadfast advice, I was able to deliver Love Rhapsodies to you and gain a new tenacity for my work. Last but not least, I want to pay respect to Mother Earth and the mindful moments of joy we receive every day. These joyous moments, our close encounters with the sky, sun, wind, earth and rain. My energy is shared with you in my writing, I appreciate you accepting my humble gift.

Inspirational Word Art

I grew up in a poor part of Essex, where Ford Motor Company expanded in South East of England. Living as a minority in a family of five children, with a different cultural experience at home, I knew respecting diversity was important and would be imprinted in my behaviour, so I grew with an open mind.

My mother always said that I was a sharing and very caring child of all her children; these birth gifts from my mother and grandmother created an open heart. Sacred Heart Comprehensive RC, my high school experience is where I learnt many hymns, studied Shakespeare and poetry with Irish and English Literature teachers. Such experiences grew my artful mind, spiritually and gave me purpose. My teachers helped pave my career and future career path as a pharmacist and adjuvant faculty professor at FAMU, UF, NSU, PBA and other schools of Pharmacy. Having a direct influence on people through my words of guidance and encouragement as a preceptor and career coach, I found myself using catchy phrases subtly to engage patients and students in taking healthier steps.

With spiritual guidance from the heavens and the serenity of nature, I learnt to express creatively for myself, through a daily mantra and poem. These were my healthy steps for mind and body at a time when healthcare providers and frontline workers had worked many extra hours often not reimbursed and overlooked by corporate executives in all fields of the industry.

My influences are poet Rumi who connected the spirit and love with the universe, and poet Li Bai, who wrote about intense love, sorrow in life, friendships, and romance centuries ago in his rhapsodies.

Their words resonate with people all over the world centuries later. These poets used their word art to create joy, peace, love, and faith in a culturally diverse world. Rumi, was he Afghani, was he Persian, was he Turkish? Was he Muslim, was he Christian, how did he define himself? Li Bai, a Sichuan poet of mixed parentage, wrote essays and poems in his style following no order, and unlike many other Chinese poets, he wrote passionately and often offended higher-ranking officials. He persisted with his art and style through most of his life, always seeking the dream of royal approval.

Both poets were able to use their poems to make friends with new people who had a different culture or provincial language. Li Bai, in 700 AD, experienced many troubles that we all face in finding our career paths, it was slow and not what he expected. He was of mixed parentage, speaking his mother's language, he used this skill to prevent conflict with different ethnic cultures in China. His belief in his writing and hope for more success with his vice, a few glasses of wine, helped his poetry echo in the minds of generations of people.

Rumi allows love to flow from the universe, Allah, God, Tao, Jesus, and Jah into your heart when you allow yourself to be open and see the world with love, peace, and feel your place within the harmony of His creation, Earth.

Beloved Buddhist Monk Thich Nhat Hanh inspired me with meditation poems. My first memory was after the birth of my daughter, I had not slept for many days and picked up his book in Barnes and Noble, "Peace is Every Step" for my self-regeneration. Reciting the words "Peace is every step, the red shining sun is in my heart."

In this moment, I walked outside whilst it rained lightly, and the sun was shining in sunny Florida. I felt peace, love and joy from the heavens blessing me with my daughter, the rainwater cooling my fatigue and the sun bright in the sky sharing warmth.

My poem writing evolved to have purpose inspired by Li Bai, Rumi and Thich Nhat Hanh, who rejoiced life, love, faith and people.

Poems are my expressions of moments of pleasure in the garden on earth, we humbly step each day embracing our soles on the earth, we can create peace in every step and tranquillity in our minds. Creating a visual auditory digital book is a modern way for me to share my experience with you, your family and work family.

My aim is to encourage word art creation in you, where you share your experiences of life, love, and mindfulness. Word art allows you to be brave and open to creating word tapestry. Words grow love, unity, and compassion in your own home, make your own tapestry. Let your words resonate like the sound of piano chords, or a guitar, bringing joy through song and music.

Your word art maybe simple, use it to foster relationships and lead people in your team.

Awaken

Morning wakens, you are here,
Hovered over my shoulder,
Sweet melodic voice in my ear,
Walked, talked, shared moments,
I felt your presence when you weren't there,
Spirit like, you love and protect,
My angel.

Balance of Love

I gift you love in this stone,
Smooth stones placed at your feet,
You can step on these while I hold your hand,
Balanced in the walk of love.

Birth

I would take the sun out from the sky,
Stop the earth from turning,
So, I could hold you in my arms,
Remembering the day,
Rubbed your delicate palms,
Tethered invisible cord,
Snuggled close you heard my heart beat,
I knew love for the very first time.

Celebration of Colours

Illuminating, celebrating,
Essence of light,
Casting shadows light, dark
Shimmering on lakes.

Paint the sky with strokes of sunlight, shades of sunset gold,
Brings peace in creatures,
Celebration of colours.

Warm glows, creating stillness in the air,
Cool tranquillity,
Calming sounds,
Birds nesting,
Rabbits are burrowing.

In your arms secure,
Your contrasting light skin and scent,
Golden glow of the sunset on your face,
Streak of fire in your eyes,
Warm soft lips,
Desire of you grows deeper in me.

Celestial Spirit

Calling the Spirit Love,
Travel like light from a distant shimmering star,
Far away in the universe beyond my knowledge,
Awoken me from a sleeping dying heart,
Sprinkled hope,
Tingling feelings spread over my naked body,
Like a flourishing free-flowing spring,
Breasts aroused,
Quivering desire,
Spell bound,
Anticipation of more,
Celestial Spirit transcends to stars.

Crimson Canopy

Charming my senses,
Vibrancy surrounds me,
Looking up, your friendly boughs are strong,
Flowers hypnotizing, dangling, I am breathless,
Alluring me to smell and kiss, I reach, I try, so high in the
crimson canopy.

The light of the morn shimmers on dewdrops on your
leaves,
I watch you swaying in the wind,
Feathered leaves delicately waver,
Wind blows like a trumpet,
Propeller petals fall down low,
Make patterns on the green like royal silks,
Lavishly wrap me in those!
Subtle fragrance of you lingers; I close my eyes, my hearts
see you,
Crimson canopies imprinted in my mind.

Daisies and Dandelions

Delicate daisies around her neck,
Made them with my hands,
Chasing butterflies, hiding behind hedges, walking on the
way,
Splashing and paddling by the lake.

Eating on the meadow, under the shade of oak,
Resting heads together as sun sets.
Warmth on faces, secret smiles in heart.

Twirling dances like the autumn leaves fall,
Walking, wading in the puddles after rain,
Playful anticipation of winter.

Dance of Green Willow

Green Willow pays homage to the earth,
Kissing caressing the soil,
Dangling his locks of green, long leaves,
Green Willow sways in the southerly wind,
Skimming and dipping the surface water,
Dissolving woes of heartache within the flowing stream.
Breeze aggravates these loving locks in bursts of dancing
anger, jealousy, another face of love,
Green serpentine glides.

Green Willow dances and calls,
Eager to impress the lovers as they pass by,
Lovers pause and gaze at the flowing locks,
Flowing, blowing over noses and smiles,
Alluring lovers to sit close by.

His green locks flow with the air,
His boughs open,
Lovers' arms securely hold,
He always bows humbly in finale, like a ballet,
Romantic audiences nod.

Dream Walking

Imagine your beautiful feet
Step slowly one, two, three,
Soles embrace the moist green grass,
Place one foot then the other,
Soles slowly,
Embrace the earth,
Soles slowly,
Embrace the earth,

Soles stepping to a warm spring,
Musical flourishing spring water,
Soles slowly,
Embrace the water,
Soles slowly,
Embrace the water.

Flow Like Water

Flow with water,
Sway like the palm leaves,
Bend like bamboo.

Seek pleasure in peaceful water,
Calmness in stillness,
Feel warmth of the sun on your skin.

Observe the slow drifting clouds,
Shapes and colours changing,
Understand skies changes, hearts change.

Love like butterflies who visit flowers,
Each encounter memorable,
Be a butterfly flying in the breeze.

Flowing Springs

Waiting by the flowing waters,
Hoping your feelings flourish,
Reminiscent of your generous love.

Fresh feelings,
You bring me to life,
Was like a withering tree that needed support.

Rooted deep in your heart,
Mingled with your thoughts,
You ponder liberating love imprisoned for so long.

Waiting by the flowing waters,
For you to drift near me,
Reminiscent of your affection,
Come to thee.

Following Lover Moon

The drunk professes his heart, when lover is not here,
Time clocks no longer tick when you are far,
Hearts beat slowly,
Sleep never fulfills,
Sustenance cannot feed hunger, belly knotted in pain.

Love drifted like clouds far away, drink Love's potion!
Taste food and live life again, again,
Dance drunk under the benevolent moon, following the
Sun.

In despair when my lover is not here,
Endlessly following like Lover Moon.

Freedom to Write

A freedom to express,
Share feelings with the world,
Liberates myself,
No longer restricted,
Mentally free,
Unlocking my own chains with poetry.

Gardener Thoughts

Twilight, a blanket of woven clouds, mirrors,
In thy endearing bosom, slumber the birds and squirrels,
deep in their sweet dreams.

Sitting in the shape of a palm tree,
Watching the ripples in the lake and feeling the gentleness of
the breeze which caresses through my whole body.

Hope

Under the luminous moon,
Beneath the quilt of stars,
Between the shade of palm,
There is light.

Even in the unknown,
In a moment of despair,
In the whistling winds,
There is light.

Celebrating a new day,
Singing at the break of dawn,
Creatures small know there is light.

If I Were a Tree

Mild fragrant air,
Gently blows in breeze,
Stirring a tapestry of silk strands,
Ballerina arms show my elegance,
Gracefully alluring eyes.

Proudly, gracefully I have stood so long,
Watched children circle around me,
Singing, skipping hand in hand,
Hands on my trunk feeling my heart.

Best nest, raindrops fall,
Mosses grow all over my skin,
My roots are deep, if you stand close you can feel my
thoughts,
I share my heart with you.

Invisibility of Love

When the skies are open,
When the heart no longer fears,
You will be ready to see me.

When you close your eyes,
When there is no light,
You can always feel me.

When my heart beats,
I breathe in deep,
I miss you dearly.

Cradled in your love,
Safe in your arms,
Your invisibility cloak supports me.

可爱的水
Lovely Water

Flowing music,
Refreshing sound,
Generously flowing streams,
Cleanse,
Fulfill,
Regenerate.

Less Love

Looking empty but wanting to say,
No words to convey,
Loss of love,
Anger surfaces, the fearsome face of Love.
Love flees,
No joy is left,
Life missing, with less Love.

Let's Close Our Eyes

Breath in deeply,
Inhale,
Exhale,
Relax your shoulders,
Place one palm on the belly,
Place one palm on the heart,
Listen with your ear on right shoulder,
Listen with your left ear,
Bring awareness to your breath,
Breathe in slowly, fill your lungs,
Feel your heartbeat,
Thank you, heart, for loving,
Imagine your feet, stepping slowly,
One step, two step,
Slowly, pausing
Soles embrace the wet grass, the wet sand,
Slowly embrace the earth,
Embrace the earth,
Embrace yourself,
Arms around yourself,
I am growing,
I am loving,
My roots grow firm,
I am safe to grow.

Life

Like a kite,
Flying and hovering in the wind.

Like the mist,
Dreamlike on lake.

Like the bright luminous Moon,
Secretly present during day and night.

Like the sunset,
A kaleidoscope of feelings.

Like the breeze,
Present and silent.

Like the cold Northern Winds,
Fierce and bitter.

Goodbye Sun,
Goodbye Moon.

Welcome rising new day,
Warming flowing energy fills earth.

Spirits speaking in dreams,
Hearts calling distant lover with no words,
Eternal energy circles,
Life love balance revolves.

Lingering Fragrance

Wind carrying forth blossom petals,
With every breath of wind, the scent of spring flowers
lingers,
Searching for flowers,
Listening to the sounds of bees,
Butterflies resting on daisies.

Budding green, pink and white,
Flowers lifting their heads high,
Honouring the sun,
Kisses in the wind, memories of love linger.

Longing for the Earth to stand still,
Rose petals fall, then the leaves,
My heart is heavy,
Birds singing in the barren branches,
Melancholy,
Sombre,
Longing for the taste of your honey.

Look, There Is Love!

Under the navy silk shimmering sky,
Under the moons revolving,
There hibernates a little love.

In the crispy snow crunching under my boots,
In the cold air that burns my lips,
There hibernates a little love.

Amongst the pine needles,
Scattered snowflakes dressing the boughs of fir,
Under the tall trunk,
There hibernates a little love.

Green grass blades grow,
Mother with her infant observes,
Snowdrop holds her floral bell,
Look there is love.

Love Lace Hearts

My friends the trees,
Forrest is abundant with lush green ivy,
Growing knitted around trunks,
Ordaining each limb of yours with a love lace heart,
Loving trees, talking roots and strong friendship,
Bringing beauty to the eyes of passing travellers,
Travellers open their hearts.

Lace heart leaves open,
Face up with no fear of nakedness,
Delicate needlework of nature,
Love laced leaves litter the path, welcome me into the
journey of love.

Love Moon Face

Joyful greetings,
Warm embrace,
Like flowering buds grateful for a new day,
Love reimagined in a new place,
Spirits connecting without words,
Memories of growing,
Laughter shared.

Like watching blooming night flowers, patiently hoping the
night never ends,
Ending, suffering separation, fractured hearts,
Anger and fear dwells sinisterly.

Wishing moon face glares, forever in navy velvet cloak,
Wishing stars eternally lighting,
Perpetual love.

Moon face is still,
Anticipating,
Moonlight illuminating hope,
Love lingers in navy velvet cloak,
Hidden.

Loving Balance

Celebrating moments,
Gushing feels of streams,
Water pounds the rocks,
Heart beats faster.

Creating moments,
Desiring your delicate kisses,
Love cradles you in the rain,
Love cradles you when you weep.

Love waits,
For blossoming,
Love wipes tears and kisses from your brow,
Reckless sometimes and heartbroken,
Distraught and fearful.

Love observes the balancing birds,
Listens to the chirping birds,
Watches and warms the chirping eggs,
Waiting for feathers to surface.

Love sounds like laughter,
Loud or timid,
Love is silent,
Love is in action,

Love is gifting affection,
Love is like honey, sweet and tempting,
Love listens, understands, reasons and sometimes not,
Love is jealous,
Jealousy anger.

Passionate embrace,
Painful farewells,
Looks of adoration across a dining table,
Lasting smiles,
Long looks, breathlessly awaiting embrace.

My Precious

She smiles and my world awakes,
She cries and I will protect her,
She binds the fabric of our family,
Inherited the wisdom of her ancestors,
She loves, she cares and is the greatest friend.

Near and Far

I wish I were your shirt so I would always feel you close.
I wish I were your glasses so I could see your eyes.
I wish I were your car as you would share mutterings of your
stresses every day.
I wish I were nomad wandering in your mind, then I would
have a home in your heart.

你在哪里
Where Are You?

Where did I see you?
How long should I look?
My heart yearns,
Pained with separation,
I think I was an appendage of yours.

Present moments flash by,
There is never enough time,
Tell the Earth to stop revolving,
I want to remain in your presence.

Like the wind I feel you;
Like the wind nobody sees me.
When you blow away the clouds in the blue sky I know of
your presence.

You create stillness in me,
Pauses and thoughts,
So helpless and I am in need,
To hear your breath,
Kiss me softly, rub noses,
Where are you?

Parchi

If you share your meal,
I will give you a parchi.
If you share words of affection, I will write on the parchi,
If you let me walk through your thoughts, I will draw a key
on the parchi,
If you repay my kindness, I write, with love, my friend on
the parchi.

Penny for the Wishing Well

Helping stepping stones across the stream,
Cool waters wash your feet of trouble,
Birds singing for you every day,
Windy days so bamboo flutes play.

Clear blue skies and warm sunsets,
Eyes feasting on natural art,
Baby rabbits eating the flowers you planted,
Fragrant burst lingers on your tongue; wind blows through
mountain flowers.
I wish your eyes to capture the mountains,
A loved one carries your weary bags, making burdens lighter,
Footsteps to friendship refills you with energy and love.

Precious

Floral crowns raise their heads,
Leaves face up to the light,
Majestic energy illuminates,
Jasmine fragrance lovingly lingers,
Mutterings of love under my breath.

Precious princess walks with grace,
Earth kisses her feet,
Her ringlet hair catches the wind,
Her eyes flutter like butterflies.

My precious is full of joy,
Mindful in the beauty of living,
She dances and paints a love footprint,
Invisible real love impresses my heart.

Quiet Spaces

In silence, I gift you my voice.
In a dim lit room, I gift you my sight.
In your loneliness, I gift you my love.
In despair, I gift you hope.

In affectionless moments, I gift you my hands.
Smoothing, caressing your skin like a gentle breeze.
Flowing hair to shade your eyes from the light of morn',
Healing kisses that strengthen.

I declare my love's name!
The Sun and Moon hears;
Stars know of our love.

Restless

Thinking, waking,
Warm, firm, skin pressing,
Kisses on my neck,
Smoothing my breasts, kissing nestling.

Nestling, rubbing noses,
Massaging hands,
Kissing abdomen,
Fragrance of lavender lingers in my hair.

Shading you from morning sunlight,
Capturing your senses in my realm,
Silky flowing long hair brushes your face,
Nestling noses,
Soft lips.
Eyes closed, hearts open, we see each other.
Bare and close, we feel each other.

Serving Love

Formally waiting for your arrival,
His large hand folded over the other as he sits,
My eyes lowered,
Heavy teapot on hot coals,
Fire illuminating the room,
Flames reflecting on His face.

Heart beats,
Lips parted, I ask if he would like tea,
He nods,
Pouring tea for you is the only pleasure I can give you,
I will enjoy the moment,
He allows me to serve you,
I bring joy,
He relishes tranquillity.

I adore Him.

Symphony of Bamboo Flutes

Bamboo so strong, still bends in the wind,
Bamboo beautiful, simple, sturdy,
My friends the trees they look sturdy and silent,
Peaceful in their tranquillity, full of life without uttering a
word,
I hear soft low tones as the wind blows, rustling long leafy
strands.
I close my eyes and listen to the symphony of bamboo
flutes.

Tonic of Life

Invigorates warmth in the cold hearts,
Brings smiles and laughter the tonic of life.

Flow in abundance,
Call out her name,
Save yourself from flames of hate, the tonic of life.

Heals deep wounds,
Washes worries,
Consoling teas, the tonic of life.

Rejoice friendship,
Raise your glass,
Celebrate living with the tonic of life.

If I Would Be a Bird

You would be the tree,
We would rendezvous.

I would whisper to wake you;
I would make home in your boughs;
By autumn leaves, I would love you still.

Loving for a season,
Goodbye my beautiful tree.

Scented air lingers even when you are bare;
You stand through the wind and rain,
Finding a new way to bloom again,
New birds nesting in your arms.

Treasures in a Trinket

A little laughter,
A few smiles,
A few longing looks with me,
Empty spaces,
Lonely nights,
Let there be few.

Discover yourself.
New friendships flower,
Fragrantly flourishing poppy fields,
Throw flowers in the wind,
Remember the souls.

My secret treasures,
Memories treasured in my heart.

美好的天空
The Good Sky

Silhouettes dancing in moonlight,
Silently sharing secrets,
Faceless like the celestial moon,
Longing for secret places.

Secrets shared, gifts received.
Life revolves under the celestial sky;
Clouds blanket the earth;
Noor's blanket energizes life;
Warmth incubates the fetus;
Love is reborn.

Under the Tree of Affection

Invitation to love under the shade of me, the tree.
Rusty leaves fall like confetti.
Falling for the earth, my heart sinks in despair,
Longing to touch,
Longing for affection,
Longing for lips.
Honey and salt tasteless without the elixir of love.

Eyes wide in dream, lean in close.
Come sit with me, Aphrodite calls.
Breeze blows his hair; fears blow into the wind.
Fresh feelings land in his heart,
Skin warmth, love fevers, forgetting woes.
He wraps his love in layers of affection,
Healing bandages,
Bosom close.

Walk of a Nomad

Journey to the unknown,
Walking behind the dunes of sand,
Scalded souls.

Parched, hungry,
Eyes sandy,
No place to rest and call home.

Nights are cool,
Moon full,
Contemplating the day's walk.

Where to go?
Walk with wife;
Sink in sand;
Tent's shelter for a night.

Eat together,
Dance and rejoice another moonlight,
Fulfilled with the unknown.

Wandering Steps

Steps wandering through a path in life;
Journey to the emerald hills,
Grasses green, streams flow,
Birds sing,
Only Hao Tian hears your thoughts,
You share silently,
The good sky listens,
Your wandering steps grow closer to know your own heart.

Waterwheel

Listening to the water flowing,
Seeing water splash,
Curiosity catches my attention,
Water droplets in my hand.

Circling fresh water,
Half full, half empty waterwheel hands,
Reflections of my thoughts,
Self-reflection within.

Creaking, cracking wheel turns,
Waterwheel hands weathered,
Wounded hands broken with time,
Farmlands drier, crops smaller,
Farmer fixes waterwheel hands,
Oxen steer while sun sets.

Sun becomes evil,
Moon becomes my friend,
Eyes pained with sorrow,
Silence is a pleasure,
Contemplation.

Revolution of hands,
Evolution of thoughts,
Solutions for my wounded affection.

Welcoming Woods

Hanging catechins,
Draped garlands,
Welcoming you into the enchanted woods.
Imperial Oak Tree stands.

Windy Day Thoughts

Breezes blowing, bringing warm caressing air,
Rustling through the grasses,
Swaying the boughs of trees,
Spreading ripples on the water, spreading calm through my
mind.

Blowing through my hair,
Stroking my silky strands, I am loved by nature,
Peaceful moments you create with those pauses,
Stillness in the air.

I enjoy warmth of sun on skin,
You blow hard,
Your cool breath on my parted mouth.

You Will Be So Far

I want you near,
Silently my heart throbs,
Mind wanders,
Eyes long to capture affectionate moments.

If I could be the sun, I see you always, keep you warm.
If I could be the rain, I always will bring joy to life.
When I am the wind, I will caress and kiss your face.
I will be the moon, watching you sleep well.

Intentions of the Day

Honouring my eyes, closing them and creating a mental image, I enjoy reflecting on "The fractured moon", a visual Li Bai described in a poem.

I imagine what this looks like, creating a vivid image, iridescent, glowing yellow-white magnificent moon. The full moon fractured, broken, just appears that way carried by the ballerina arms of the barren tree. The tree now poses a beautiful fractured moon, I close my eyes focusing and contemplating the beauty of the moon. I breathe and rest my eyes using my imagination to generate this mental picture, sometimes the moon is reflecting in the water, ripples of the moon shimmer on the dark navy water. The moon brings serenity in my thoughts and I feel this in my meditation, I hold the feeling for as long as I can.

I enjoyed writing these poems for people who are able to read, I hope that those who cannot are able to ask a friend to read for them. My intentions were to share my word art to a global audience who all suffered during the pandemic. Things may seem different in this post COVID era, however the desire for art, freedom and simplistic joy is appreciated by all humans that walk on mother earth.